Skiing Basics: All About Skiing

ISBN-13: 978-1479274703

ISBN-10: 1479274704

Copyright Notice

All Rights Reserved © 2012 Dani Beekley

SKIING BASICS:
ALL ABOUT SKIING

Dani Beekley

I dedicate this to the lucky people who've been touched by the joy, excitement and buzz of skiing...

Contents

The History of Skiing

Before it became a sport, skiing was used as a means of traversing snowy terrain for thousands of years.

Some people say the oldest skis ever recorded were the ones found near Moscow, which were deemed to be around 4500-8000 years old.

However, there are also those who believe the oldest skis in the world were the ones found in Sweden, which were dated back to 3200 BC.

Still, other people point to the fact that there are some rock carvings in Norway depicting scene where men used skis and these carvings possibly date back even further.

It was in 1933 when the very first rock carvings with men on skis depicted were discovered in Norway.

In 2001, other carvings were discovered in another part of the country.

So far, there have been more than 200 prehistoric skis discovered in different parts of the world, most of them in the marshy areas of Norway, Russia, and Sweden.

These skis are now being brought to laboratories for carbon dating so as to ensure accuracy in testing. In the past, testing for these skis was done by pollen testing methods or with the use of other organic material. However, those methods were much less reliable and accurate.

Even Norse mythology has references to skiing when gods and goddesses were said to have hunted while using skis as a means of travel.

There are also texts that mention Onduris, the goddess of skiing, as a name attributed to the goddess Skade, as she's known to be the finest skier among all the gods.

Until now, cross country races are still being held regularly in Sweden and Norway in celebration of the early accounts of skiing as part of medieval life.

Skis used to be designed for gliding over flat surfaces until the 1700s, when skiing is recorded to have grown more refined and skis started being used not just for practical purposes, but also for sport.

This was when people began skiing downhill and used jumps as a recreational activity rather than for purely logistical reasons.

Sondre Norheim is said to have been the one who first designed binding from wet birch, which gave better grip to the shoe and provided the skier with more flexibility when making turns.

Because the original skis weren't made for downhill skiing or jumping, this marked a new era in skiing.

In 1932, the very first Birkebeiner Run was held in Norway to commemorate a ski run that's believed to date back to 1205 AD and this event is still being held annually until now.

The difference is that the event now involves a combination of cross country skiing and mountain bike racing, with both races carried out with a 3.5kg backpack.

The popularity of skiing increased even more after World War II.

By the 1950s, skis started being manufactured from metal rather than the original wooden models with metal edges.

Quick-release bindings were also invented to reduce injuries and lightweight poles were introduced, thus changing the way turns are made on ski slopes.

Ski resorts in the United States then began offering lifts and hotel services. Soon, snow-making machines and slope-combing units came into the picture as well.

Today, skiing has indeed become much safer, but still as exciting as ever.

Tips for Beginners

Skiing is one adventure sport that has much to offer in terms of fun, speed, and thrill. This may be why a lot of people flock towards the mountains during the winter season in order to engage in this sport.

And it's not even just the long-time skiers who flock to ski resorts each year. There are also those who are learning the sport for the very first time. This clearly shows just how popular the sport has become over the years.

If you've also become interested in the sport and are planning to learn some skiing moves either for recreational or sporting purposes, then you'll surely appreciate the following tips on how you can glide smoothly along the slopes.

If this is absolutely the first time you're ever stepping onto a ski slope, then it would be wise to rent your skis rather than buying them. After all, this is still a sort of trial period to see if you will indeed enjoy the activity or not.

Other than the skis, you'd also do well to rent ski gear and equipment, including the ski helmet, gloves, and goggles.

The value of renting your equipment and gear for starters lies in the fact that these are quite expensive, so it isn't very practical to buy them at the outset when you're not yet sure if you'll ever be using them again or not.

Once you've actually tried the sport and found that you enjoy it and are likely to become a regular skier, then that's the time you should consider buying your own skiing equipment and gear.

As you rent a pair of skis for the first time, it's advisable for you to make sure the skis you choose are about 30cm shorter than your own height. That is the length that'll provide you with just the right grip and a good balance.

Take note that if you fail to get the length of your first skis right, your very first skiing experience is likely to be spoiled and you just might not find it as enjoyable as it can actually be.

When you choose your ski shoes, you should also make sure they're comfortable and lightweight enough.

Your toes should still be able to move inside the shoes, but you should also make sure the shoes aren't too loose that your feet actually lift off of the base when you walk.

Once you've put on all of your protective gear, including your ski helmet, gloves, and goggles, you need to take a few minutes to see if there's anything broken, loose, or even just a bit uncomfortable.

Remember that anything of this sort will likely reduce your enjoyment of the activity and increase your risk for injury. Taking just a few minutes to ensure everything is in place can do much to reduce the likelihood of accidents occurring on the slopes.

Furthermore, it helps you avoid getting distracted by relatively unimportant matters. It's very important for you to have the right set of ski helmet, gloves, and goggles so you can truly enjoy your time on the slopes.

Choosing a Ski Jacket

So, you've decided to take up skiing. In that case, one of the things you need to buy is a ski jacket.

Take note that the task of buying a ski jacket involves more than just picking out a piece of clothing that's stylish comfortable.

Although it's definitely advisable to choose a ski jacket that fits your personality and sense of style, it's even more important for you to make sure the jacket has a number of practical features as well.

Among the most important features you should look for when shopping for a ski jacket is waterproof or water-resistant outer shell.

There can be nothing worse than getting weighed down on the slopes by a waterlogged ski jacket.

The good news is that practically all ski jackets are designed with waterproofing. And if you want to achieve flexibility with your ski jacket, you'd do well to choose one with a removable lining.

This makes it possible for you to use the jacket in both cold and warm temperatures. When you go out on a nice sunny day when there's no wind chill, you could simply remove the jacket's lining and then you're ready to go!

A jacket's lining should also be breathable so as to let excess moisture and body heat escape. Look for a jacket that has air vents in strategic places and zippers that allow you to close the vents on colder days.

Take note that a ski jacket isn't meant to be form-fitting. The ideal ski jacket is, in fact, about one size larger than what you normally wear.

This is because skiing requires you to dress in layers, which means you would add or remove layers of clothing depending on the outdoor temperature. This helps ensure that you don't become either too warm or too cold as you ski.

Wearing a larger jacket lets you wear multiple layers of clothing comfortably. In fact, it would be wise for you to wear a few layers of clothing when you try on ski jackets so you'll get a good idea of how well each jacket will fit when you're out on the slopes.

One feature that's commonly overlooked, but can actually be very convenient, is a set of zippered pockets. After all, you'll need a good place to store your keys, money, identification, and other important things when you go out to ski.

Naturally, you wouldn't want to place these things in pockets where they can easily fall out, which is why you need zippers.

Of course, you'll want to make sure the jacket you choose has zippers of good quality so you won't have to struggle in trying to open or close them after just a few months of use.

It's a good idea to give each zipper a few test runs to make sure they operate smoothly and don't get caught in the fabric of the jacket.

You'd also do well to choose a ski jacket that features a hood. Many people also tend to take this feature for granted, but it can be quite handy.

While a hood isn't really necessary for keeping you warm, since you'll likely be wearing a ski hat for that purpose.

However, a hood will definitely be very useful in case of a snowstorm, as it can provide you with added protection from the wind and snow.

By keeping these tips in mind, you'll be on your way to finding the ski jacket that's just right for you.

Choosing a Helmet

There are two main reasons why it's important to protect your head when you go skiing.

First, this reduces the likelihood of suffering from injuries that may cause some serious damage to your head. Second, it helps protect you from the cold and keep you warm as you ski. You therefore need to choose a suitable helmet before going out on the slopes.

Among the first things you should take note of is that a ski helmet is entirely different from cycling helmets. They're designed specifically to protect you from the usual hazards associated with skiing. These helmets are typically insulated to protect you from the chill and their design also provides adequate protection to your forehead.

Here are the components and features you need to look for in a ski helmet:

1. Impact Resistance

Make sure the helmet you choose has a hard outer shell that's capable of absorbing shock, withstanding strong impact, and resisting scratches.

Its design should be such that the effect of shock is evenly distributed over the whole shell so you can avoid feeling intense pressure in one part of your head in case of a collision.

The helmet you choose should have an appropriate liner that can protect you from serious brain injuries.

A good helmet liner is one that compresses in a fall so as to maximise protection and then expands by itself.

If the lining remains compressed after a fall, you need to discard it immediately and look for a new one.

2. Ventilation

The helmet you choose should have enough ventilation. Take note that you're likely to collect a considerable amount of moisture on your face and head as you ski.

The presence of moisture could make it a bit uncomfortable for you to keep wearing the helmet and may even become a cause for distraction while you ski.

This is why it's important to choose a ski helmet with a sufficient number of vents for proper inflow and outflow of air.

3. Fitting

You should make sure the ski helmet fits your head just right. For one thing, there shouldn't be any gap between the top of your ski goggles and your helmet.

It's important for the helmet to have the ability to protect your forehead, so it has to be positioned right above your ski goggles about an inch from your eyebrows.

It may be a good idea to buy your ski goggles and helmet at the same time so you can try them on simultaneously.

You also have the option to use interior sizing pads for a great fit.

These are the most important things you need to look for when you start shopping for a ski helmet.

By choosing the right ski helmet, you'll be able to enjoy the activity even more as you're assured of your safety while skiing.

Of course, there are several other things you need to do and precautions to take in order to reduce the risk of injury, but wearing the right ski helmet has much to contribute towards that end.

Choosing Ski Boots

In order to get the right ski boots, you first need to understand what a boot fitting is all about.

For one thing, bear in mind that fitting for ski boots doesn't just involve choosing colours and graphics and then having someone measure your foot size to "fit" your boots within just a few minutes.

That kind of fitting will only have you ending up with uncomfortable ski boots that could become a distraction on the ski slopes.

Always remember that the fitting process for ski boots has a lot of difference from fitting for hire boots.

One of the first things you need to do when you decide to go for a boot fitting for skiing purposes is to set aside enough time for the process.

On average, this could take about 30 minutes, but may sometimes last longer.

In fact, a boot fitting could last for two hours if you have very specific requirements.

Here's the general boot fitting process you'll have to go through:

1. Interview

A good fitter sits down with you and spends a few minutes just talking.

He should ask about your skiing style and if you have any issues with your lower back, your legs, your knees, your feet cure, or anything else.

Your feet usually have to cope with a lot of things and it can take very little for any problem to go from your feet to other parts of your body. A good fitter doesn't proceed to the next step until they gain at least a basic understanding about you.

2. Analysis

A good fitter will spend a few minutes analysing your feet before doing the actual fitting. He is likely to use a Podoscope, which emits a blue light fired under your feet and allows you to see what's going on.

Some fitters also use a thermal plate to draw the outline of your feet. The fitter will then observe your stance to see if there's canting or bowing in your legs, particularly in relation to your hips and knees.

From these observations, a profile of your feet will now be drawn up along with measurements of your feet's width and length, and a determination of the volume of ski boots that need to be fitted.

3. Fitting

Finally, you'll be made to try on a few pairs of boots until the fitter finds one that's best suited to your foot profile as well as your personal requirements.

Once the right pair is identified, the fitter will make insoles specifically designed for your feet based on the first two steps. These insoles are then inserted into the boots and you'll probably be offered coffee as you wait for the boot liners to be heated up and moulded.

You'll then be asked to try the boots on and walk around for a few minutes to see if it feels comfortable enough.

If there are any issues, the boots will be brought into the workshop for the necessary adjustments. The fitter will then refit, recheck, and repeat if needed.

Whatever you do, you should never choose ski boots based on brand and colour alone!

Simply by devoting enough time to proper boot fitting, you can enjoy having a pair of boots that'll help improve your skiing performance.

Choosing Goggles

You probably already know how important it is to wear the proper gear when you go out skiing.

For this reason, you're probably careful about wearing your pads and ski helmet whenever you go out to enjoy the sport.

But, if you're like most people, then you probably often take for granted the importance of ski goggles.

You may not realise it, but wearing the right ski goggles can make a lot of difference in your performance as well as your skiing experience.

This is especially true since lens technologies have come a long way in recent years from photo chromic lenses to interchangeable lenses.

It's easy enough for you to find a pair of ski goggles that's suitable for all types of weather conditions.

There are, of course, a number of things you need to take into consideration when you shop for a pair of ski goggles.

Among the things that skiers consider very challenging is the task of identifying a white object that's lying on the equally white snow.

And the task of adjusting to visual changes in fast-paced and snow-covered environment can be just as challenging. These are instances when the right pair of ski goggles can come in very handy.

These goggles are offered in a wide variety of colours that help increase contrast and improve visibility as well as depth perception, particularly under changing lighting conditions.

Bear in mind that different lens tints are suitable for different lighting. Orange tints are ideal for skiing in sunny to moderate weather conditions whereas amber and gold are advisable for skiing in low to moderate lighting conditions.

Brown and gray are the best options for bluebird days, while rose and light yellow are best suited for skiing on gray or overcast days.

Helping you identify objects in a snowy landscape isn't the only benefit offered by ski goggles. Take note that your eyes can be harmed by overexposure to UV rays, even on cloudy days.

When you're in high-altitude areas such as ski resorts, the intensity of UV rays is higher than usual and you're likely to suffer from a condition known as snow blindness.

And considering the wide expanse of snow you'll be traversing when you ski, you can understand that there's a serious risk of harming your eyes.

In fact, research has shown that snow has the ability to reflect up to 80% of the UV radiations it encounters.

Imagine what that can do if it gets reflected directly into your eyes! It's therefore vital for you to always have your ski goggles on while you're enjoying a skiing adventure.

A number of manufacturers have also come up with ski goggles equipped with a fog dissipation feature, which helps provide you with a clear view of your surroundings even in extreme conditions.

Another important consideration is for your ski goggles to be compatible with your ski helmet.

This is to avoid discomfort that can be a cause for distraction when you ski. It may even be wise for you to buy your goggles and helmet at the same time so you can try them on together.

Choosing Your Skis

Every skiing enthusiast has to go through the task of buying his first pair of skis.

If you're just starting out, then you're actually quite lucky because you can make use of the wealth of information about skis online, in sports magazines, and even from friends who have been skiing for some time.

A pair of skis is a huge investment, but it can bring amazing payback as long as you make the right choice.

The most obvious advantage of having your own skis, of course, is that you won't have to waste time waiting your turn at the ski rental queue. Here's how to choose the right pair of skis:

Type of Ski

The very first thing you should do towards getting the right pair of skis is to determine what type of skier you are as well as the type of skier you hope to become.

This is because there are different types of skis and they suit different types of skiers as well. Here are the basic types of skis:

1. Piste Skis

As the name implies, this type of ski is best suited for skiing on piste and in good snow conditions. These skis are excellent carvers and there are models that use the same technology used in the racing scene. The drawback is that they're likely to struggle a bit when you go off-piste or ski in less than perfect conditions.

2. All-mountain Skis

This type of ski allows you to enjoy the sport in different snow conditions. Regardless of whether the snow is slushy or icy, these skis will still perform better than piste skis. The drawback is that it tends to lose a bit of carving ability unless you choose to buy higher end models equipped with the latest technology for maintaining carving ability.

3. Back-country Skis

This type of ski is best for hiking all over the mountain, as they're typically versatile enough to use out of bounds and much lighter than other skis, thus making them easier to carry uphill.

These skis usually don't come with their own bindings so you'll have to choose the appropriate bindings according to your needs.

4. Off-piste Skis

This type of ski is ideal for skiing in off-piste conditions and on powder. They're typically wider and a bit more forgiving to allow for more feel in powder. It also allows for the absorption of impact during jumps and landings.

Length of Ski

Once you've determined the type of ski you need, you'll have to find out what the right ski length is for your needs.

The key factors in choosing the length of your skis are your height, weight, and skiing ability.

The general rule is that a ski is too short if it reaches below the tip of your nose when held upright. If it is taller than you, then it is too long.

There are, of course, exceptions to this rule, which is why you need to take your weight and ability into consideration as well.

A good ski store should have a sizing guide that'll help you choose the right ski length.

Indoor Skiing as a Prelude to the Real Thing

Whenever skiing is mentioned, many people automatically think it should be done outdoors and can only be enjoyed during winter when the mountains are blanketed with snow.

That may have been the case in the past, but because of human ingenuity, it is now possible to ski indoors whenever you want.

There are now a number of indoor ski facilities that allow you to enjoy the sport all year round.

In fact, there just might be such a facility near you and you're simply unaware of its existence.

This may be the first time you're learning about indoor skiing and you may be wondering why you should try it instead of going directly to the real thing.

Well, the truth about indoor skiing is that it really doesn't have that much difference to outdoor skiing. You still get to ski down a slope and you still get to feel the cold from a snowy ground.

Perhaps the biggest difference is that the "snow" in this case is produced by machines rather than by nature.

The good news is that this artificial snow can't be considered inferior to natural snow in any way.

In fact, a number of these facilities are designed so professionally that they're even used in official competitions.

So, now that we've taken care of the quality issues, here's another significant advantage of trying indoor skiing: Indoor ski facilities offer the most benefits to those who are experiencing the sport for the first time.

Take note that skiing can be a dangerous activity primarily since you're going down a mountain slope at a very quick pace.

Since indoor facilities are considerably more forgiving than outdoor slopes, it'll be much easier and safer for you to learn how to ski in an indoor facility. This is because the surface of indoor slopes is specifically to absorb falls more effectively.

Furthermore, indoor slopes are understandably more predictable than outdoor slopes, so you know exactly what you're dealing with.

Another obvious advantage of indoor skiing is that you get to enjoy it at any time of the year.

For obvious reasons, many outdoor ski resorts are open only during the winter. But, because they're self-maintained, indoor skiing facilities are typically open all year round.

This means you can enjoy the skiing experience even during the hot summer months. There are, in fact, many professional skiers who use these indoor facilities so they can train for the sport all year.

As a beginner, you can use such a facility to master the basic skiing techniques so that when wintertime comes, you'll be confident enough to start hitting the outdoor slopes.

There's indeed a good reason for adrenaline junkies getting hooked to indoor skiing.

It allows them to enjoy the thrill of the skiing experience any time of the year and they can do so while being a lot safer to boot! Indoor skiing can indeed be the best precursor to the real thing.

Practice in safety to gain confidence in skills and then go ahead and hit the outdoor slopes. Have fun!

Joining a Ski Club

Since you've taken interest in the sport of skiing, you may have heard about ski clubs and may even have been advised to join one.

As a result, you may now be wondering if doing so is indeed necessary and what possible benefits it can offer you.

Well, no one can really decide whether joining a ski club is a good idea or not, but yourself.

To help you make that decision, it would be best for you to learn more about how you can possibly benefit from joining a ski club.

One of the benefits of belonging to a ski club is that you get access to a number of specific perks.

These perks tend to vary from one club to another, but in most cases, they're likely to involve registrations and access to ski slopes, among other things.

Such perks may also include discounts in such things as entrance fees, ski rentals, hotel accommodations, etc.

A good number of these ski clubs also offer an exclusive and comprehensive insurance policy that covers each of their members, thereby protecting them in the event of an accident. You may not really have thought about insurance when you first decided to learn how to ski, but it's actually something of a necessity.

Being part of a ski club also brings a certain exclusivity with it. As previously mentioned, members typically get to enjoy exclusive perks.

Beyond the perks, however, you get to enjoy exclusivity in terms of your social profile as a skier being significantly raised.

If you're part of a ski club that automatically means you'll be with like-minded individuals who share your passions and interests.

And depending on the profile of the club you choose to join, your membership could even lead to new contacts within the skiing scene.

Still another huge advantage of joining a ski club when you're just starting out is that it can be an excellent training ground.

As a newcomer to the skiing scene, you naturally want to learn the ropes of the sport. What better way for you to learn, then, that to be with people who know exactly what they're doing?

Learning can even go beyond the high-level supervised training members of your club can share. Those who've been skiing for some time could also show you the proper way of carrying yourself as a skier.

You could also learn about important things such as safety and interacting with other skiers on the slopes.

So, how do you get to become a member of these ski clubs?

Well, you'll likely be asked to take care of a membership fee, which needs to be paid either annually or monthly.

There may also be some specific requirements for membership, but once you get in, you officially become part of an elite group of skiers.

At the very least, you get to become part of a group of like-minded individuals who can help you grow considerably and quickly as a skier.

Now that you're aware of the benefits of joining a ski club, you're in a much better position to decide whether this is indeed the right thing for you to do.

Safety Tips

If you've never engaged in winter sports before, then you may be wondering if there's any difference between skiing and snowboarding.

Well, these two activities are practically the same, except for the fact that skiers use skis and snowboarders use snowboards.

Where the task of ensuring your safety is concerned, however, there's a world of difference between these two outdoor activities.

Of course, there are also similarities, such as the fact that skiers and snowboarders alike are required to wear helmets and ski or snowboard only within the limits of their abilities.

And just like in any other sport, the basic rule is for you to always stay alert, be attentive, and be prepared.

Winter sports such as skiing have become increasingly popular in recent years. And as the number of people participating in these sports continues to increases the number of injury cases has also increased.

The most common type of skiing injuries is head injury, which accounts for over half of the cases of death due to accidents associated with winter sports.

Wrist injury is the second most common type of injury suffered by skiers in different parts of the world. In every skiing season, there are approximately 10,000 incidences of wrist fractures in North America alone.

The best way you can avoid any form of injury that may be caused by skiing is to take lessons from a professional.

In these lessons, you'll be taught about the intricacies of skiing, including the art of falling with your hands held in a fist position.

Research has shown that the use of protective gear such as helmets, ski gloves, wrist guards, and the like can reduce the risk for injury by about 43 percent.

Here are a few tips on how you can avoid wrist injuries, in particular:

✓ Take skiing lessons from an experienced ski coach. A good coach will not only teach you how to ski, but also how to board and fall without hurting yourself.

✓ In case you fall forwards, strive to fall on your forearms rather than your hands. If you fall backwards, try to let your buttocks take the brunt of the fall and refrain from trying to protect yourself with your hands.

✓ Every time you fall, try to hold your hands in a fist instead of opening them. This offers you a bit of support and prevents your fingers from splaying out. A good pair of ski gloves could come in handy in these instances, as it can cushion your hands and reduce the risk for injury. Some ski gloves are even equipped with built-in wrist guards.

✓ Use your forearms so your wrists are kept stable and prevented from hyper-extending.

✓ Put your forearms down to protect your face and keep it from hitting the ground.

- ✓ Be sure you use the right ski equipment and gear. Make sure your ski gloves, tailbone pads, wrist guards, knee pads, elbow pads, helmets, etc. all fit properly and are of good quality. You may also want to consider buying a combo pack or ski gear set to avail of discounts on quality items.

- ✓ Keep yourself in shape at all times. Skiing is one sport that requires much in terms of physical fitness and you'll surely be able to enjoy it more if you're in good shape.

Fitness Training for Skiing

Skiing is an extremely strenuous activity when done for recreational purposes, more so when you undertake it as a competitive sport, regardless of your chosen variation (cross country, slalom, downhill, etc.).

This is the reason why you need to work hard in ensuring that you're in good enough shape to meet the physical demands of the sport in terms of balance, speed, and agility.

This makes it highly important for you to engage in ski fitness training.

Ideally, you need to undergo at least eight weeks of ski fitness training before you even set foot on the slopes.

Your aim at this point should be to build muscular strength and develop maximum endurance, particularly in your legs.

Just like you would with any other fitness training programs, you should always remember to warm up properly before launching into the bulk exercise component of your training.

Gentle stretching during your warm-up session should sufficiently prepare your body for the intense activity to follow as it stimulates blood circulation and initiates the secretion of bodily fluids that help feed your muscles and lubricate your joints.

Make sure you start stretching from the top of your body and then progressively work downwards without any rush. It should take about ten to fifteen minutes for you to complete your stretches.

After the stretching session, you'd do well to spend fifteen to twenty minutes on the treadmill at a pace that's somewhere between a fast walk and a slow jog.

Basic cardio training like this one strengthens your heart and helps lower your bad cholesterol levels, while also improving your overall lung function at the same time.

Take note that ski fitness training has to simulate the actual type and extent of physical activity involved with skiing as closely as possible.

It is therefore a good idea for you to consider including exercises such as skipping rope in your ski fitness training program.

This type of exercise not only improves your blood circulation, but it also sufficiently conditions your knees into constant bending.

At the same time, it helps you develop strength and endurance in your thigh muscles.

Skipping rope is a lot faster than jogging, so it also effectively exercises your "fast" muscle fibres. This allows your legs to respond quickly to the undulating conditions of a ski slope.

Finally, it would be wise for you to include weight training in your ski fitness program.

When you do so, be sure to focus on lower intensity with high repetitions, since your aim is to tone and condition your muscles and develop endurance, rather than to build bulk.

It's also advisable to use free weights instead of fixed weights in this case. This allows you to gain a better balance and coordination as your core strength increases, thus stabilising your trunk and spine.

By following the tips discussed above, you may well be on your way towards improving your skiing skills and avoiding serious injury at the same time.

Naturally, you'll have to reinforce your fitness training with proper nutrition.

There isn't a specific recommended diet for skiers and it's best to consult a professional nutritionist for developing the most suitable nutrition plan to complement your ski fitness training.

Basic Skiing Tips

The task of learning how to ski may seem a bit daunting, but you shouldn't be discouraged. Skiing can be an excellent sport for you to learn. It's a lot of fun, it's exhilarating, it helps you burn a lot of calories, it requires skill, and it takes you to some of the world's best mountain locations.

One of the keys to learning how to ski is your equipment. Although you don't really need to spend a fortune, it's also ill-advised to just go with the cheapest equipment you can find.

Doing so could make it more difficult and much less fun for you to learn the sport. What you need to do instead is buy a ski hat of decent quality, a good pair of ski gloves, a scarf, some ski socks, and thermal pants.

For starters, you may rent ski boots, skis, and poles at the ski resort. Now, you're ready to learn the basics of skiing.

1. Standing on Skis

The first thing you need to do, of course, is learn how to stand with your skis on.

As you try to get off the ground after putting on your skis, make sure you're facing the side of the slope rather than downhill to avoid going down the slope sooner than you expect.

2. Proper Stance

This may seem obvious to those who've skied before or watched a lot of skiing events, but many people are actually unaware that you need to bend your knees and then lean slightly forwards. Life on the slope will be much harder if you fail to do this.

3. The Snowplough

Once you're able to stand comfortably and take the proper stance, it's time to start moving downhill. Towards this end, you need to keep your knees bent and then push your weight forward as you face downhill.

If you want to come to a stop, you need to point your toes in and then push your heels slightly outwards. If you happen to cross your skis, just lift the top ski up with your foot and then try the manoeuvre again.

If you feel yourself starting to panic and you badly want to stop, all you need to do is sit down.

4. Making a Turn

Making a turn involves turning your feet towards your desired direction. This may sound easy, but it actually takes a bit of practice. This can easily be done in the snowplough position and then you can proceed to parallel turns when you're confident enough.

Face the direction you want to go without looking at your skis, as that might make you lose track of your position on the slope.

Take note that a huge part of skiing has to do with confidence. You need to know your limits and ensure safety at all times, but remain confident in your skiing ability.

Once you lose confidence and start to panic, that's when you're likely to fall and that's something you surely wouldn't want to happen.

Improving Your Balance

Balance is one of the key components to becoming a good skier. Improving your balance is therefore an excellent way of improving your overall performance on the slopes.

Having good balance also effectively increases your confidence in your skiing abilities and as you probably know by now, skiing is about confidence for the most part.

One good way to improve your balance is by engaging in exercises that enhance your overall muscle strength, especially since skiing is a physically demanding sport.

Here are a few of the balance exercises you may want to consider incorporating into your ski fitness training routine if you haven't done so already:

1. Single Leg Deadlifts

The first exercise on the list works by strengthening your glutes, your hamstrings, and your lower back while improving your balance at the same time.

When you execute this exercise, try to think of lifting with your glutes instead of pulling through your back so you can achieve the best results.

2. Single Leg Split Squats

The second exercise you may want to include in your workout routine works by targeting your hamstrings, quads, and glutes. This is also an excellent exercise for improving core strength. When you perform this exercise, be sure to maintain an upright position throughout the movements. Doing so will help prevent the development of lower back pain and ensure that you're targeting the right muscle groups.

3. Lateral Raise on One Leg

The final exercise on the list works by strengthening your shoulder muscles. Now, what does it have to do with balance, you say? Well, the fact that your working your shoulders while standing on just one leg boosts your balance quite effectively.

To maintain a good muscular balance, you have to make sure you perform the exercise in an equal number of repetitions for both sides.

It's best to do two sets of ten to fifteen repetitions on both sides.

These are just three of the best exercises that can effectively improve your balance and subsequently improve your performance in skiing as well.

Start incorporating them into your ski fitness training sessions and you'll be sure to see some significant results in no time at all.

Remember that your ability to ski begins and ends with your ability to maintain good balance with your skis on.

This is why you need to constantly work on improving your balance, especially if your ultimate goal is to compete in major skiing events.

As your balance improves, you're likely to notice that you have more control of your movements on the ski slopes as well. As a result, you'll be more confident the next time you zip down those slopes.

And once you're assured that you have excellent balance, you may even grow confident enough to start learning some ski tricks, which are essential in most skiing competitions.

So, why wait? It's best to start working on those exercises and seeing your balance improve now. You'll be sure to thank yourself for doing so in time.

Improving Core Agility

As you begin training to become a good skier, you should also continue working on your ski fitness training routines.

These routines are, in fact, excellent ways of boosting your performance and helping you avoid possible injuries.

Remember that skiing can be very physically demanding and may even put you at risk of getting injured in a number of ways.

This makes it all the more important for you to make sure you're in good enough shape to withstand the physical demands of the sport.

The good thing about ski fitness training workouts is that they don't necessarily take too much time to perform, but they can have a huge influence on the level of your skiing skills.

One particular aspect of your physical fitness that you need to address with your training routine is your core strength.

Be sure to engage regularly in exercises that boost your core strength, as this is essential to staying injury-free when you hit the slopes.

Here are some of the best exercises that can help you improve your core agility and strength:

1. Lying Leg Raise with a Twist

The first exercise on our list is ideal for targeting your oblique muscles as well as your upper and lower abs. This will also help improve your muscular endurance. To perform this exercise, lift your legs straight up ninety degrees and then slowly shift them to the side as far down as you can go while still maintaining control over the movement pattern. Once you've lowered your legs to their limits, reverse directions and then repeat the movement on the other side.

2. Pike on a Ball

The second exercise on the list is also an excellent exercise for improving agility because it requires you to use the exercise ball. This exercise also helps improve your shoulder strength.

To perform this exercise, place your feet on the exercise ball and your hands on the floor beneath you. Contract your abdominal muscles such that you form an inverted V.

Hold this position for a second and then stretch back out into the full position. Pause briefly and then repeat the exercise five to eight more times.

3. Reverse Crunch

The last exercise on our list is ideal for firming up you lower abs and ensuring that you're able to maintain constant tension in your core while you ski.

To perform the exercise, you need to lie flat on the floor with your legs bent and then pull your legs into your chest as hard as possible.

Pause briefly and then reverse the movement pattern to complete one repetition.

Do ten to twelve repetitions, rest, and then repeat the exercise.

By adding these exercises to your ski fitness training routine, you'll surely notice some significant core strengthening benefits that help reduce your chances of getting sidelined due to injury.

If you're serious about building a career in competitive skiing, then you need to be serious about getting in shape for the sport. Skiing may look easy, but it can be a tough sport unless you're fit enough.

Basic Tricks for Beginners

Once you've become comfortable with the basic skiing skills and developed the ability to execute them with confidence, you may want to start taking your skiing skills to the next level.

Since, you're now confident about sliding along those snow-covered slopes, you may start practicing a few of the basic skiing tricks that are easy enough for beginners to learn.

These basic tricks are typically performed as you fly through the air and just before you land. Of course, learning and executing these tricks don't just involve wearing the appropriate ski clothes, a ski helmet, and mouth guards.

They also require adequate knowledge of the proper techniques in order to ensure safety.

Furthermore, these tricks require patience and constant practice before you even dare to perform them on the slopes.

Before you even start practicing any of the basic skiing tricks, make sure you've already mastered the basic ski techniques.

These techniques include falling gracefully, executing a kick turn, and side slipping, among others. Make sure as well that you have impact shorts and mouth guards on before trying any of the basic skiing tricks.

As soon as you've taken all of the necessary precautions, you can start learning the freestyle skiing tricks.

Here are two of the most basic tricks you may want to try:

1. The Daffy

This trick is executed by extending your legs in a split while you're up in the air. Perhaps the most important consideration for those who want to try this trick is that you should have mastered jumping off the slope first.

And when you jump, you should have a fair idea of how high above the ground you are before you perform the split. Again, there's a need to emphasize the importance of wearing impact shorts and mouth guards to shield you from injury in case of a fall.

Now, here's how a daffy is executed: As you jump off a slope, you need to extend one of your legs in front and the other leg at the back to do the mid-air split. Make sure you jump high enough into the air before doing the daffy so you'll have enough time to bring your legs back together as you land.

2. The 360

As the name implies, this skiing trick involves making a complete 360-degree turn in the air. Your main focus in executing this trick should be on making a safe landing after performing the turn. As soon as you take off from the slope, you should turn both your shoulder and your head towards the desired direction of your turn.

And the moment you make your turn in mid-air, you should already have a general idea of when, how, and where you're going to land. Make sure you land in such a way that you're able to bear the impact well.

These are just two of the basic skiing tricks you may want to learn as your confidence in your skiing skills grows. As soon as you master these two tricks, you can start practicing other basic tricks or even more advanced skiing tricks.